HORSES AND
PONIES

HORSES AND PONIES

by Julie Richardson
illustrated by Libby King

Willowisp Press

Published in 1986 by Willowisp Press, Inc.
401 E. Wilson Bridge Road, Worthington, Ohio 43085

This Book Fair Edition published by arrangement with
Granada Publishing Limited
London, England

Copyright ©Granada
American Text Copyright ©1986 by Willowisp Press, Inc.

ISBN 0-87406-091-5

Printed in the United States of America

10 9 8 7 6 5 4 3 2 1

Granada ©
Granada Publishing ©

Contents

The Horse

The earliest known type of horse was on earth 60 million years ago—millions of years before man. The horse was first used by man about five thousand years ago. But it was many years later that man began to breed horses to suit his own needs.

Points of the Horse

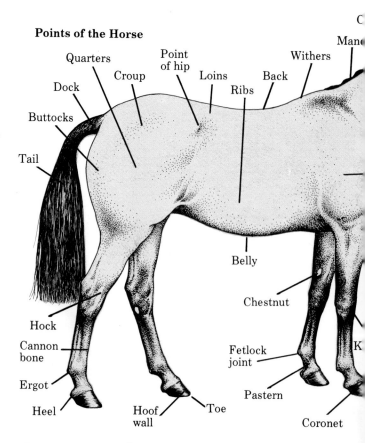

C

Mane

Quarters

Point of hip

Withers

Croup

Loins

Back

Dock

Ribs

Buttocks

Tail

Belly

Chestnut

Hock

Cannon bone

Fetlock joint

K

Ergot

Pastern

Heel

Hoof wall

Toe

Coronet

Horses today are a combination of the needs of nature and men. Nature changed the horse to be large, strong, and single-toed with a hoof. Man could select nature's best horses, and breed them to establish the best characteristics possible.

This continues today in breeding farms all over the world. In fact, only one species of purely wild horse is still in existence. It is the Mongolian Wild Horse, better known as Przewalski's Horse.

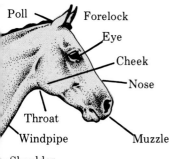

To be able to judge a good horse or pony, it is essential to be able to identify all "points" of the horse and note their relation to one another in a well-made animal.

At first, men kept horses for food. Soon they realized how useful horses would be pulling carts and plows and carrying loads. Once the art of riding was mastered, men rode out hunting and into battle with speed they had never thought possible. Horses pulled carts on farms and carriages in towns. Sports on horseback—jousting, racing, jumping, polo—have attracted enthusiastic participants and audiences since medieval times.

Today, horses are still used for work and for giving riders pleasure. There are many reasons why the horse has long been known as "The Friend of Man."

7

Good, Bad, and Ugly

Conformation simply means "the shape of the horse"—how he is "put together." Horses, like people, are built differently. This affects the way they perform, how strong they are, and how long they will be able to live an active life. Some conformation defects can actually make a horse unsound. Having an eye for a good horse is an art. But it isn't hard to learn how to spot particular points to avoid. Any of the defects, shown on the horse below, should be avoided.

At first glance, the horse should look good, being nicely proportioned and balanced. Rather small heads, with ears to match, and big, bright eyes are best. Broad foreheads denote intelligence. Coffin-shaped heads are merely ugly, but wide eyes indicate unpredictability and bad temper.

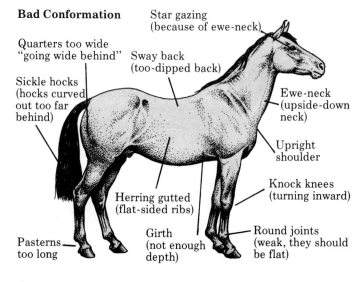

Bad Conformation

Star gazing
(because of ewe-neck)

Quarters too wide
"going wide behind"

Sway back
(too-dipped back)

Sickle hocks
(hocks curved
out too far
behind)

Ewe-neck
(upside-down
neck)

Upright
shoulder

Knock knees
(turning inward)

Herring gutted
(flat-sided ribs)

Pasterns
too long

Girth
(not enough
depth)

Round joints
(weak, they should
be flat)

Face Markings

1 Blaze—white marking from the forehead down the face to the muzzle. **2** Snip—isolated white mark between the nostrils. **3** Stripe—similar to blaze, but narrower. **4** White face—white covers the forehead and nose in a broad band down to the muzzle. **5** Star—any white forehead mark. **6** Walleye—white or blue eye, caused by lack of iris pigment.

Shoulders should have a good slope. Chests are best broad, backs short, girths deep, and quarters nicely rounded. A goose rump (jumper's bump) is said to mean that the horse can jump well. A narrow chest puts the forelegs "out of a hole," which is bad.

Good legs and feet are very important. Both pairs of feet should match in size and shape. The feet shouldn't be too flat or too upright. Long pasterns denote weakness. Short pasterns may cause strain and also give an uncomfortable ride. Cannon bones should be short. Knees and hocks should be of flat bone.

Unsoundness and bad habits

Horses must be sound to perform well. Good lungs are important. Lumps and bumps on the legs may cause problems. Bone spavins—bony lumps on the side of the hock—are particularly bad. Those on the splint bone should not give trouble unless they interfere with a joint.

Bad habits include biting, kicking, rearing, napping (refusing to do as told), bucking, weaving (waving the head from side to side), crib-biting, and windsucking.

Colors and Markings

A horse's color is that of his coat (body color) and points (mane, tail, lower legs—apart from white hairs—and muzzle). His markings are the white hairs on the face and lower legs. The two most common white body markings are saddle marks—white patches under the saddle—and girth marks, which are white patches under the girth.

1   2   3   4

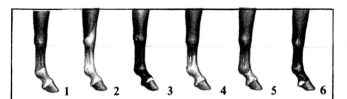

Leg markings
1 Sock 2 Stocking 3 Coronet 4 Fetlock 5 Pastern
6 Heel. White leg markings covered with black dots of hair
are called "ermine."

The five main colors are:
bay, black, brown, chestnut,
and gray. The horses shown
below are:
1 Gray
2 Liver Chestnut
3 Bay
4 Iron Gray

5 Chestnut
6 Piebald
7 Strawberry roan
8 Palomino
9 Spotted
10 Dun
11 Skewbald
12 Black

5   6   7   8   9   10   11   12

Horse and Pony Types

Many horses and ponies are purebred and are entitled
to be registered in their breed's stud book. This book
lists pedigrees for many generations and helps to
ensure that the breed remains pure. One of the biggest
stud books in the world is for the Thoroughbred horse.
Most riding horses and ponies, however, are not purebred. They are a blend of breeds and become known
more for their type than their breed. A purebred
animal may also be a type (a Welsh Mountain Pony is
a riding pony, for example) but a type of animal does
not belong to any particular breed.

Riding Pony
Ponies bred today are really "riding ponies." Pony breeds
include the Shetland, Welsh, Hackney, Connemara, and
Dartmoor. Some of the best ponies are part-Thoroughbred
or part-Arab.

Polo pony

Usually, ponies are between 13 and 14.2 hands. Many—particularly those with mostly horse blood—are very pretty. Others are plainer, but perhaps more sensible. They can be trained, making good pets for children.

Polo Pony
Polo ponies are still called "ponies," but they are now all over 15 hands and some are more than 16 hands.

A good polo pony must have courage. It should be fast, obedient, and quick to change direction. A long neck, good shoulders, and powerful quarters help make a fine, wiry pony and a good goal scorer.

Most polo ponies are Thoroughbred. The best, which come from Argentina, are bred from cow ponies and Thoroughbreds. They play with a built-in sense of the game and bring big prices.

Cob
Cobs are honest, down-to-earth little horses, renowned for their strength, stamina, and good temper. Ireland and Wales produce probably the best types. They are common in England.

Cob

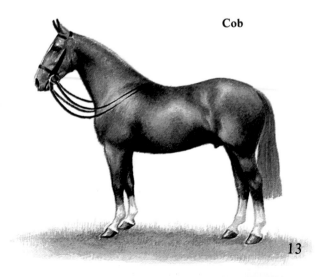

The cob has a big body, rather short legs—particularly below the knee—and is no higher than 15.3 hands. Heads are rather big, but these should be proud rather than ugly. Necks are powerful and arched, backs are short. Girths— the width and depth of the horse—are wide, giving a lot of area for the heart. Cobs carry their tails high. Manes may be cut short.

Hunter

Any horse or pony can be ridden out to hunt fox or stag. But a true hunter is a recognized type of horse.

It is a quality, strong animal, up to weight with a deep, short body and strong legs with good bone. Height ranges from 15.3 hands to 17 hands.

Many show hunters are Thoroughbred. Most hunters used in the hunting field are crossed with such breeds as draft horses or the bigger ponies.

A good hunter should have the courage and stamina to hunt two days a week. It should stand quietly when necessary, gallop, jump safely, and not pull too much. It must also

Hunter

ignore hounds—kicking a hound is the worst thing a hunter can do in the eyes of the master.

Hunters are usually associated with Britain and particularly with Ireland, where superb hunters are bred.

Hack

The hack is a light riding horse of any breed, but usually Thoroughbred, Anglo-Arab, or part-bred Arab.

The name was first coined in Britain. A covert hack was an elegant horse used to carry its master to the hunt meet. A park hack was even more elegant, small-boned, and was used by society ladies and gentlemen for pleasure riding.

Today, the show hack must still be beautiful and well-mannered. It must have great presence, a light mouth, and straight, elegant action. Its conformation must be as near perfect as possible, with no unsightly blemishes such as splints or swellings.

Hacks do not exceed 15.3 hands. They are often ridden sidesaddle in the show ring by women.

Hack

Horses of the World

Arab

The Arab is the most beautiful horse in the world. It is also the oldest breed—probably over 4,000 years—and the purest. It has given its beauty and strength to every other breed, including the Thoroughbred.

The Arab's dish-shaped face and high, bannerlike tail are legendary. But the Arab also has a short, strong back, sound legs and lungs, and can carry much heavier loads than its size suggests. Arabs are mostly chestnut, bay, or gray. Arabs are fiery but kind, and are used as all-around riding horses. An Arab crossed with a Thoroughbred is called an "Anglo-Arab."

Arab

Thoroughbred

Thoroughbred

The Thoroughbred is the fastest horse in the world. Its well-proportioned frame has made the Thoroughbred famous all over the world.

It was bred first in England more than 250 years ago from three Arabian stallions crossed with European mares. Like the Arab, it has since been crossed with other breeds to pass on its qualities.

The Thoroughbred is a top-class light animal with a refined head, elegant neck, good sloping shoulders, hard legs, and strong quarters. It is high-spirited and sensitive.

Usually it stands between 15 and 17 hands. It may be brown, bay, gray, chestnut, or black.

Britain

The mountain and moorland ponies which originated in the British Isles are seen all over the world. There are nine major breeds.

Dales
The sturdy Dales ponies are small versions of heavy horses. They have a lot of feather (hair) on their heels, strong, short legs, compact bodies, and short necks topped by elegant pony heads. They are used for riding, but are also good driving ponies.

Exmoor
Exmoors are the purest native ponies, not unlike the original wild horses. Their foreheads are broad, ears short and thick, and nostrils wide. They are well-known for the unusual hooded "toad" eye and thick double-haired coat. They make tough, but independent riding ponies.

Dartmoor
Dartmoors are good-looking ponies, rather refined, and generally good riding types. They have the surefootedness and sense of good moorland breeds.

Dales
Height: up to 14.2 hands.
Colors: black, dark brown, gray.

Fell

Fells are the lighter brothers of Dales ponies. They make sensible riding ponies and are widely used for trail riding.

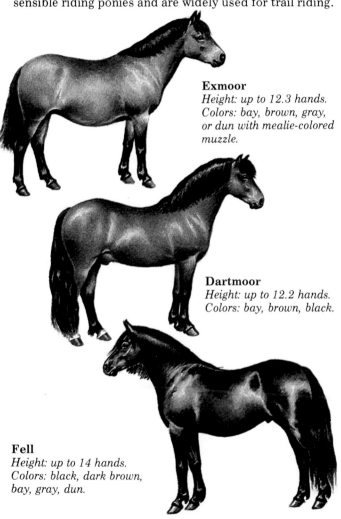

Exmoor
Height: up to 12.3 hands.
Colors: bay, brown, gray, or dun with mealie-colored muzzle.

Dartmoor
Height: up to 12.2 hands.
Colors: bay, brown, black.

Fell
Height: up to 14 hands.
Colors: black, dark brown, bay, gray, dun.

New Forest
Of all the British ponies, the New Forest is the most mixed in its blood. Most New Forests have good substance and compact necks, but plain heads are common. Usually, they have good legs and feet.

Connemara
From western Ireland come the attractive Connemaras. These are hardy and sound, intelligent and kind. They are natural jumpers and make excellent cross-country ponies.

Highland
From Scotland come the biggest and strongest natives, the Highlands. They are large-bodied ponies that are still used to carry shot deer. A lighter type is found in the western islands.
Height: up to 14.2 hands. Colors: dun, black, bay, gray, all with dorsal stripes.

Shetland
Shetlands are the smallest ponies in the world—and the strongest in relation to size. They learn quickly, are gentle,

New Forest
Height: up to 14.2 hands.
Colors: any but piebald and skewbald.

20

and are international favorites for children's riding. They have distinctive small heads, compact bodies, short legs, and thick manes and tails.

Height: up to 42 in (106.6 cm). Colors: black, brown, bay, piebald, skewbald.

Welsh

Welsh ponies are divided into four types, called "sections." Welsh Mountain ponies are Section A and are probably the most popular and the most beautiful. They have lovely dished-shaped faces, small muzzles, and large, intelligent eyes. They move quickly and freely on strong legs and hard feet. The Section B Welsh Pony is bigger than the Welsh Mountain. The breed is a mixture of Welsh Mountain and the larger Section C Cob. They are full of quality, and are known as the finest riding pony in the world. They make superb competition ponies for children. Section C Welsh Cobs are general-purpose ride or driven cobs, bigger and stronger than Welsh Mountains and with the fine trotting action of the good cob. They also jump well. Section D cobs are the biggest of the four Welsh breeds. They are famous for their versatility as riding and driving cobs.

Connemara
Height: up to 14.2 hands. Colors: gray, black, bay, brown, dun.

Welsh Mountain Pony
Height: up to 12 hands. Colors: any except broken colors.

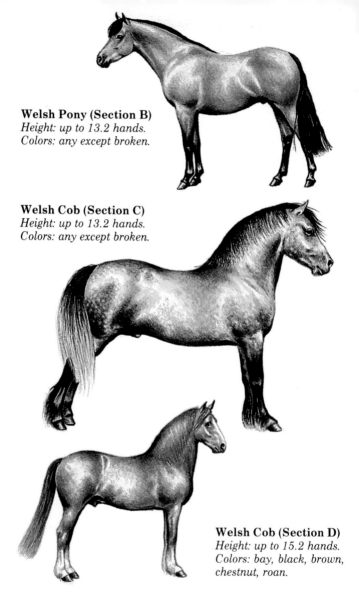

Welsh Pony (Section B)
Height: up to 13.2 hands.
Colors: any except broken.

Welsh Cob (Section C)
Height: up to 13.2 hands.
Colors: any except broken.

Welsh Cob (Section D)
Height: up to 15.2 hands.
Colors: bay, black, brown,
chestnut, roan.

Hackneys

Hackneys are descended from the Norfolk Trotters. They come from the flatlands of East Anglia, England. Most are related to a horse called Matthias, who lived nearly a century ago.

Hackneys have a marvelous high-stepping trotting action that is striking. They lift their knees high and suspend each foreleg for a moment at each stride. Then they thrust forward from their hind legs.

Hackneys are mainly driving horses. They are seen all over the world on farms and in the show ring. They are bred with thick withers, high head carriages, and longer backs than most other horses.

Height: up to 16 hands. Colors: bay, brown, black chestnut, often with white stockings.

Hackney Pony

Hackney ponies are treated as a separate breed. Besides horse blood, they have connections with trotting ponies from Westmoreland, England. They look like small versions of Hackney horses and move the same way. They have vibrant personalities.

Height: up to 14.2 hands. Colors: same as Hackney.

Hackney

The Heavies

Shires, Clydesdales, and Suffolk Punches are the best-known British heavy horses. All three are big and powerful draft animals. They are used on farms, and are favorites in parades and horse shows.

Shires
Shires are probably the biggest horses in the world. Often, they weigh more than one ton. (See picture, page 56.)
Height: up to 18 hands. Colors: black, gray, brown, bay.

Clydesdale
Clydesdales are exceptionally active for their size, with particularly strong feet and lower legs. Heavy feather is on the legs.

Suffolk Punch
Suffolk Punches are also active and clean-legged, with little feather on the heels.

Clydesdale
Height: up to 16.2 hands.
Colors: bay, black, brown,
roan.

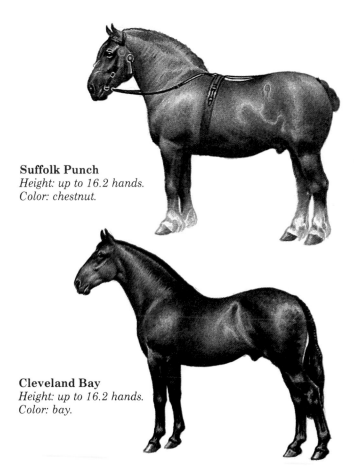

Suffolk Punch
Height: up to 16.2 hands.
Color: chestnut.

Cleveland Bay
Height: up to 16.2 hands.
Color: bay.

Cleveland Bay

The Cleveland Bay is a very old carriage-drawn breed from Yorkshire, England. These good-looking horses have large Roman noses and small eyes. They also have long necks and nicely sloping shoulders running into deep chests. As well as pulling carriages, they are used for farm work and general riding. They are crossed with Thoroughbreds for a lighter type of hunter, show jumping, or event horse.

North America

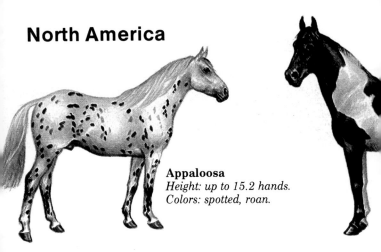

Appaloosa
Height: up to 15.2 hands.
Colors: spotted, roan.

Appaloosa

The Appaloosa is one of America's top breeds. They are the best-known spotted horses in the world. They were developed as war horses by the Nez Perce Indians of Palouse, Idaho, and are now riding horses and circus performers. They are compact, with strong quarters. Their skins are pink and the spots stand out as if they are embossed.

Morgan

Morgans are famous light horses. They originated from a horse born in 1790 in Vermont, named Justin Morgan. They are very strong—particularly in the shoulders and neck—and neat. Intelligent and willing, they are used for pleasure riding, showing, driving, and even in weight-pulling contests.

Pinto

Pintos are also famous American Indian horses. They are called "pinto," which means "painted," because of their piebald and skewbald coloring. They have been a recognized breed for nearly 20 years, but don't have any particular conformation, temperament, or size.

Pinto
*Height: varies,
about 14 hands.
Colors: piebald,
skewbald.*

Morgan
*Height: up to 15.2 hands.
Colors: bay, black, brown,
chestnut.*

Tennessee Walker

Developed in Tennessee in the 1850's, Tennessee Walkers are said to be the most comfortable and amiable horses in the world. They get their names from an extra gait—a half-walk, half-run glide along the ground that the rider hardly feels.

Tennessee Walker
*Height: up to 15.2 hands.
Colors: black, bay, chestnut.*

France

Ardennais

Ardennais horses are short-legged, but massive-framed animals once used as heavy cavalry horses. The breed is one of many French draft, some others being Percheron, Boullonais, Breton, and Comtois. Ardennais are hardy, thickset horses that are particularly docile and easy to manage. They are popular in Belgium, Sweden, and Poland, as well as in France.

Ardennais
Height: up to 15.3 hands.
Colors: bay, chestnut, roan.

French Saddle Horse

Once called "Anglo-Norman," the French Saddle Horse is a mixed-blood breed. It is well-known for producing competition and army horses. Generally, these horses are strong and nicely made, although their conformation above the knee if often better than below it. They are known in France as *Cheval de Salle Francais.*

Camargue

Camargue horses are the wild natives of the swampland of the Rhône delta in southeast France. Their distinctive white-gray color, wildness, and the way Camargue cowboys

French Saddle Horse
Height: up to 16.3 hands.
Colors: usually chestnut.

use them for herding bulls, have given them a romantic image. They have large, straight-nosed heads with eyes that are wide apart. Their great strength stems from exceptional legs and hind quarters, wide chest, and deep girth.

Camargue
Height: up to 15 hands.
Color: white-gray.

Germany

Hanoverian
Height: up to 17 hands.
Colors: bay, black,
brown, chestnut, gray.

Hanoverian

Hanoverians are a fairly modern northern breed that has become Germany's top warm blood animal. They are very strong, with exceptionally powerful hindquarters and a distinctive tail carriage. Some of the greatest show jumpers and dressage horses are now Hanoverians. A similar but heavier German breed, the Holstein, is also a good competition horse.

Trakehner

Trakehners are quality horses with a lot of Thoroughbred and Arab blood. They jump well and have great stamina, yet they are gentle riding and driving horses.

They proved their endurance in World War II. The breed was flourishing in East Prussia in 1945 when the Russian army arrived. In a desperate bid to escape, yet save the breed, stud workers harnessed unshod in-foal mares to wagons, rounding up stallions, and started a 900-mile marathon that took nearly three months. Less than a thousand escaped, but now the animals are flourishing again, both in Germany and in Poland (where they are called "Masuren").

Trakehner
Height: up to 16.2 hands.
Colors: any solid color.

Dülmen

The semi-wild little Dülmen ponies are one of the two native German pony breeds. They live on the forested land of the Dukes of Croy. They are left untended for most of the year until annual roundups.

Dülmen
Height: up to 13 hands.
Colors: all.

Austria

Lipizzaner

The beautiful Lipizzaner horses have become world-famous for their high-school (advanced) dressage performances with the Spanish Riding School in Vienna. The breed is more than 400 years old—based on the Bohemian Kladruber with Arab and Andalusian blood. Lipizzaners are highly intelligent, elegantly built, compact, and strong. They have a lot of presence combined with a calm temperament, which helps in dressage work.

Haflinger

Haflingers are Tyrolean mountain ponies bred for harness and pack work. They are strong, heavy, sure-footed ponies with short legs. They put their small heads down low to help them pull when climbing. Many still work at 40 years old.

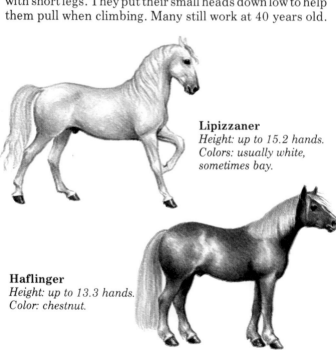

Lipizzaner
Height: up to 15.2 hands.
Colors: usually white,
sometimes bay.

Haflinger
Height: up to 13.3 hands.
Color: chestnut.

Portugal and Spain

Lusitano

The two main breeds of horse in Portugal are the Altér Real and the rather heavier Lusitano. Lusitanos are an old breed, coming from the Spanish Andalusians (see below) and still resembling them. They are often trained in high-school dressage and are used in mounted bullfighting.

Andalusian

Spain's Andalusian horses were the finest in Europe until just two centuries ago. They have proud heads and strong bodies that are particularly well-made in front. Usually, they have short backs. Like Lusitanos, they are agile and fiery. But they are still friendly and known for their high-stepping action.

Lusitano
Height: up to 16 hands.
Colors: usually gray.

Andalusian
Height: up to 15.3 hands.
Colors: gray, white, bay, roan.

Denmark

Knabstrup

The descendants of this old, spotted breed are often rather plain. Their history dates back to the Napoleonic wars. They are very popular in their native country and in circuses all over the world. They are lively and good riding horses.

Knabstrup
Height: up to 16 hands.
Color: spots on gray.

Iceland

Iceland Pony

Once the only means of transportation in Iceland, these ponies are stocky and hardy. They are descendants of Irish and Norwegian stock. They live mainly in semi-wild herds. They are noted for excellent eyesight and a strong homing instinct.

Iceland Pony
Height: up to 13 hands.
Colors: dun, gray, chestnut.

Norway

Fjord

Fjords are descendants of the Mongolian Wild Horse. They are noted for their dun color, and willfulness. They are tough and muscular, with nice heads. Their ancestors were used by the Vikings for horse fights. Fjords now spend time peacefully in harness on farms throughout Scandinavia.

Fjord
Height: up to 14.2 hands.
Color: dun.

Netherlands

Gelderland
These horses belong to a century-old breed noted for presence. They have noble good looks, even though they sometimes have plain faces. Usually, they have rather short legs for their size, but they move well and are said to be good jumpers. Now, they are ridden, as well as being used for carriage and draft work.

Gelderland
Height: up to 16 hands.
Colors: bay, chestnut, gray, skewbald.

North Africa

Barb
The hardy desert-bred Barb horses are almost as much a part of North African life today as they were centuries ago. They are similar to Arabs, but less spirited. Some say they are bad-tempered, but many are roughly treated from birth. They are known to thrive in poor conditions. Obvious characteristics are the flat shoulders and sloping quarters.

South Africa

Basuto
Basuto ponies are descended from Barbs and Arabs. They were the first horses to be brought to South Africa. They are small, short-legged ponies with long backs. They carry surprisingly heavy weights. They are very hardy and versatile, and can be used as pack and riding ponies.

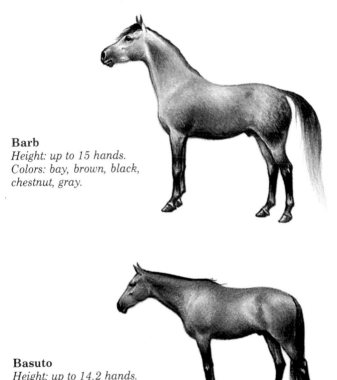

Barb
Height: up to 15 hands.
Colors: bay, brown, black,
chestnut, gray.

Basuto
Height: up to 14.2 hands.
Colors: bay, brown, chestnut,
gray.

Australia

Australian Waler
Walers are superb jumpers, and they also buck. They are a mixed-blood breed coming originally from Spain and being crossed with Thoroughbred and others. They are tougher than Thoroughbreds. Many are used by police and cavalry, and on stock farms. Others are general riding horses.

Australian Waler
Height: about 16 hands.
Colors: brown, bay, black,
gray, chestnut.

Brumby
Brumbies are the wild mongrel descendants of the early Australian settlers. Most are thought useless even when broken-in, because of their wildness.

Timor Pony
Although Timors come from Indonesia, they are well thought of and bred both in Australia and New Zealand. They are very strong and used for riding and driving.
Height: up to 12.2 hands. Colors: all.

South America

Criollo
Height: up to 15 hands.
Colors: any unbroken.

Criollo

Criollos are South America's native ponies, dating back to 1536. Criollos have had a tough existence full of temperature changes, fires, floods, and even wild dogs. It has left them as some of the toughest ponies alive. They have broad, flat-chested bodies, particularly well-muscled at the neck. Besides being tough, they are sound and good-tempered.

Falabella
Height: up to 7 hands.
Colors: any, but ideally spotted.

Falabella

Falabellas are miniature horses from Argentina. They were bred by crossing Thoroughbreds with Shetlands. They can claim to be the world's smallest horses. They are in great demand in the U.S. as a child's "first pony." They are friendly little animals, but lack strength and substance.

Riding and Care

"Gaits" or "paces" are the ways a horse moves forward. Three natural gaits are walk, trot, and canter. A fast canter is called a gallop.

Walk The walk is a four-beat gait. It is made up of four steps.

Trot The trot is two-beat. The left forefoot and right hind foot move together, as do the right forefoot and left hind foot.

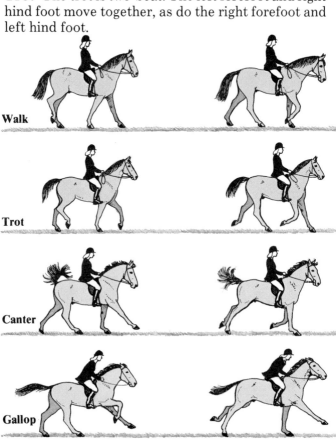

Walk

Trot

Canter

Gallop

Canter The canter has a three-beat rhythm. When moving to the left, the first leg to move is the right hind. It is followed by the left hind and right-fore, which move together. The left-fore moves last, and the horse is said to be "leading" on that leg.

Gallop The gallop is the fastest pace. It has four beats, like the walk. Each hoofbeat can be heard.

Horses are natural jumpers, but they don't jump unless they have to. Loose in a field, most will go around rather than over an object.

When a horse jumps he makes an arc over the fence in four stages: the approach, takeoff, suspension (in midair), and landing.

The approach As the horse is about to jump, he lowers his head, stretches his neck and looks down. (Horses judge the height of the fences from the groundline at the fence's base, upward).

Takeoff At takeoff, the horse shortens his neck, gathering his hind legs beneath him. He lifts his forelegs, bends his knees, and uses his forward force to push him up.

Suspension As the horse is in the air, the horse gradually unfolds his knees and restretches his neck.

Landing The horse lands on one foreleg, quickly followed by the other, and then the hind legs. His head and neck rise to balance him.

Tack

Tack is the complete bridle and saddle outfit worn by the horse. The bridle and bit allow the rider to change pace and direction. By using the seat and legs the rider can ask for flexion (the relaxing of the jaw and bending of the head).

The basic bridle is a snaffle bridle, which has a minimum of straps and fittings. It supports a single bit of any type. It may be fitted with any noseband. The plainest noseband is the cavesson. Many riders prefer to use the drop, Grakle, or flash types to stop the horse resisting the bit.

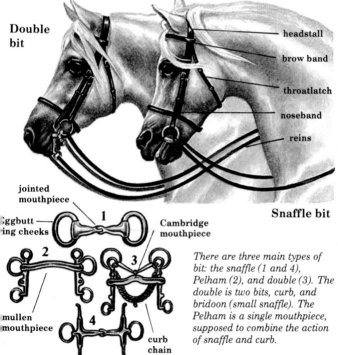

Double bit

headstall

brow band

throatlatch

noseband

reins

jointed mouthpiece

Eggbutt ing cheeks

1

Cambridge mouthpiece

Snaffle bit

2

3

mullen mouthpiece

4

curb chain

There are three main types of bit: the snaffle (1 and 4), Pelham (2), and double (3). The double is two bits, curb, and bridoon (small snaffle). The Pelham is a single mouthpiece, supposed to combine the action of snaffle and curb.

43

Most saddles are leather and are built around a skeleton of wood or metal called a "tree." The tree holds them in shape. Saddle trees are easily broken and unless mended will injure the horse's back.

All saddles should fit the horse and rider. They should not rub the horse, particularly on his withers and spine, and should be regularly restuffed. The seat should fit the rider.

Occasionally saddles, called pads, are made of felt with no tree. They are used on small ponies to be ridden by young children.

There are many types of saddles. The most common are general purpose, jumping, and dressage. They all keep the rider in the best position for a particular task.

The jumping saddle has forward-cut panels and lets the rider shorten his stirrup leathers and get his weight over the withers. The dressage saddle has a deep seat and straight-cut panels and flaps, putting the legs and seat into a good dressage position. The general purpose saddle combines features from both saddles to allow the rider to ride in both positions. Another saddle, the show, simply shows off the horse's good points. Other saddles designed for particular sports are: English hunting, side-saddle, polo, racing, and western stock.

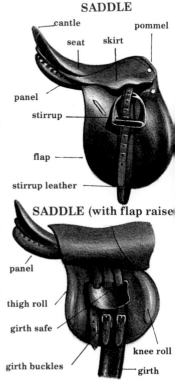

SADDLE

cantle
pommel
seat skirt
panel
stirrup
flap
stirrup leather

SADDLE (with flap raise

panel
thigh roll
girth safe
knee roll
girth buckles
girth

Other items of tack are also essential:

Halters of rope or nylon are used for leading or tying up the horse. Halters are stronger than leather headcollars, but not as attractive.

Girths are used to keep the saddle secure and there are many types: leather, string, nylon, and webbing.

Stirrup leathers must be strong or they may be dangerous. Rawhide is noted for its strength.

Stirrup irons are bought about a half-inch wider than the rider's foot so that the boot won't get trapped. Safety irons, such as the rubber-sided Peacock, break open during a fall and release the foot.

Lunge rein and whip are useful for exercising the horse in circles without a rider on his back.

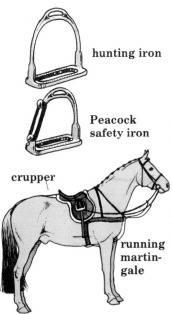

hunting iron

Peacock safety iron

crupper

running martin- gale

Caring for Tack

Clean leather daily with a damp sponge. Then soap it with glycerine saddle soap. It will look good and wear longer. Uncared-for leather gets brittle and cracks. Dirty tack may also cause skin ailments, such as girth galls. Metal parts of tack should be polished and greased, and material parts brushed or washed. Do not polish the bit.

Horse fully tacked up with snaffle bridle, general purpose saddle, breastgirth, running martingale, and crupper.

Grooming and Clothing

Grooming keeps horses healthy and improves their appearance. It removes dirt, dust, dead hair, and sweat, and tones the muscles. Usually, grooming is done daily. Ponies kept outdoors in cold weather should be given only a light brush-over, or oils that keep them warm will be removed from the coat.

Always groom a horse from front to back. You need these items:
Dandy brush *Removes caked mud and sweat.*
Body brush *Removes dirt and grease. Stimulates circulation.*
Curry comb *Metal—cleans body brush; rubber—cleans winter coat.*
Mane comb *Untangles hair in mane and tail.*

Water brush *Washes feet and dampens mane and tail.*
Sponges *One used for wiping eyes, ears, and muzzle, another for wiping dock and sheath.*
Hoof pick *Removes mud and stones from under the hoof. Must be done daily.*
Stable rubber *Polishes coat.*
Sweat scraper *Removes excess water from coat after washing.*

dandy brush

body brush

water brush

rubber curry comb

hoof pick

metal curry comb

sweat scraper

mane comb

sponge

stable rubber

Most horses wear a rug at some time. Rugs used in the stable to keep the animal warm include the stable (night) rug and the woolen day rug. In hot weather, a cotton sheet keeps the horse cool and free of flies. When sweaty, the string vestlike sweat rug keeps him warm as he dries. A waterproof canvas or nylon rug is used to protect a horse from cold, wet weather.

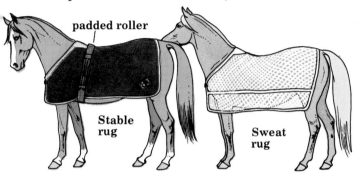

padded roller

Stable rug

Sweat rug

Boots and bandages guard the legs from injury and give support and warmth. Brushing boots protect between the knee and fetlock, while over-reach boots protect coronet and heel. Bandages offer more support and warmth. Exercise bandages are used during work; stable bandages, at rest.

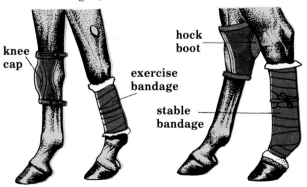

knee cap

hock boot

exercise bandage

stable bandage

Shoeing

Horses are shod to prevent their feet wearing away on modern roads and becoming sore. The horny outside wall of the foot grows in the same way as human nails. In the wild, this is worn continuously. With a shoe the wall isn't worn away at all. So a blacksmith must every month remove the shoes, scrape the horn, and replace or renew the shoes.

There are two types of shoeing: hot or cold. In hot shoeing, the blacksmith molds the red-hot iron to fit the horse's hoof before nailing it on. The familiar burning smell is produced by the hot iron singeing the insensitive underside of the hoof. Shoe varieties are shown at right.

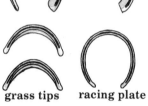

feather-edge **three-quarter**

grass tips **racing plate**

Feeding and Stabling

Most horses require 10 to 12 gallons of clean water daily. Grass is the horse's natural food. They also need salt for good health.

A horse can live on grass only when he is at his best and not doing much work. At other times, he should be given extra food, like oats and horse nuts, or hay.

When snow is on the ground, hay is given to replace bulk. Hay is simply dried grass. It is best when it is between 6 and 18 months old. It should never be brown or moldy.

Good fresh grazing and hay for horses should have a lot of "good grasses." Top quality hay is often made purely from clover, alfalfa, and Timothy. Prickly weeds should be pulled out of grazing fields to allow good grasses to grow, but dandelions and herbs can be left as most horses like them. Horses need at least an acre of grassland each if they are to remain healthy.

meadow fescue   ryegrass

Hay net correctly tied up

lucerne   red clover

red fescue   hard fescue

Grazing

Grazing horses can be healthier and happier than stabled horses. But if they are needed for heavy work, they are usually stabled so that food, exercise, and grooming are controlled. Horses are bad grazers, leaving large areas of grass untouched and souring others with droppings. Removing the droppings helps stop this, but the ideal way is to allow the field to "rest" for a few months each year by removing the horses. Fields used for horses need to be regularly checked for harmful objects which may cause injury.

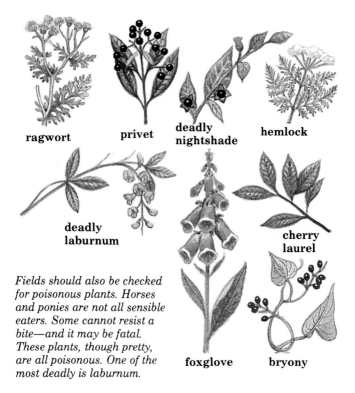

ragwort

privet

deadly
nightshade

hemlock

deadly
laburnum

cherry
laurel

Fields should also be checked for poisonous plants. Horses and ponies are not all sensible eaters. Some cannot resist a bite—and it may be fatal. These plants, though pretty, are all poisonous. One of the most deadly is laburnum.

foxglove

bryony

Hard food

Horse food other than grass and hay is called "hard food." Of all hard food, oats are the best grain. All grain should smell sweet and be clean. It is fed rolled or crushed. Barley and corn should be cracked.

Bran is a by-product from wheat milling. It is mixed with other grains to add bulk and help digestion.

Horse nuts are a prepared pelleted mixture of balanced food. All feeds may need vitamin supplements.

crushed oats

whole barley

flaked maize

bran

sugar beet

nuts

Stabling

Stabled horses rely upon their owners because they are unable to care for themselves. Every day they must be taken out, fed, watered, exercised, and groomed. If the weather is cold they must be covered with a rug.

Stalls should be light and airy and big enough. Ideal stalls are 8 feet by 10 feet or 10 feet by 12 feet. They should be ventilated so that any drafts are higher than the horse's back. The floor should be good, hard-packed dirt.

Popular beddings are straw, peat, wood shavings, and sawdust.

A stable bedded with straw and fitted with automatic drinker, corner manger, hay net fitting, and good ventilation.

At Pasture

Horses at pasture also need regular attention. They are less work than those that are stabled. They may not need routine exercise. But they should be handled daily to ensure that they are uninjured, and to clean under the hoof with a hoof pick.

In cold weather, particularly when it is wet, horses should have some shelter. An open-sided building is best, but a thick hedge may suffice.

Sometimes, an outdoor rug is necessary. This is a waterproof canvas lined with a blanket. Costly ones do not need belts or bands to keep them on.

Two patterns of an outdoor rug.

Coping with Ailments

There are many signs that show a horse is hurt or ill. Apart from the obvious ones of cuts or lameness, they include a running nose, dull coat and eyes, high temperature, refusal to eat or drink, and swollen glands.

It is often best to leave serious injuries or illnesses to be treated by a veterinarian. But minor ailments may be treated by a knowledgeable owner.

First-Aid Kit

A first-aid kit for a horse should include the items on the opposite page.

Cotton wool dipped in antiseptic diluted with warm water is used to clean wounds before further treatment. It is also used for bathing eyes and noses.

To take a horse's temperature, a thermometer is smeared in vaseline and inserted into the animal's rectum. The correct temperature is 100.4° F. (38° C).

Epsom salts in warm water draw impurities from wounds. Antiseptic powders disinfect and speed up healing. Creams are used when wounds start to heal.

Kaolin paste is made into a hot or cold poultice to draw foreign bodies from the foot or flesh.

Every first-aid kit should also contain worm powders. These are used every six weeks to rid the horse of worms, some of which can kill him.

Lameness

Horses are subject to many ailments. One of the most common is lameness. The horse will show he is lame by nodding his head down as the sound leg touches the ground. Lame horses should be still until cured.

gamgee tissue

Epsom salts

cotton wool

vaseline

worm paste

antiseptic

liniment

elasticated bandages

sulphonamide powder

gauze

colic radiol

methylated spirit

thermometer

cough electuary

scissors

glycerine

pine tar

poultice

sponge

55

Horses at Work

A Shire horse ready to pull a brewery wagon in the show ring. Heavy horse manes and tails are braided with colored ribbon.

Many horses other than riding horses work very hard for their daily oats. Heavy horses still pull farm plows and carts and draw wagons full of different things. Lighter horses sometimes find themselves in the limelight of the circus, cavalry, or police force.

Most horses are extroverts. They love to show off. That's why many of them grow to love performing before a crowd.

Circus

There are two main types of circus horses. Liberty horses, which are often part Arab, are the well-trained, high-school horses that do circus performances equivalent to dressage. The level-backed, smooth-cantering Rosinbacks calmly bear the weight of circus artists' somersaults and other antics.

Police

Police horses are chosen for size, strength, and amiability. Highly disciplined, they are trained never to kick, even when under attack. They are used for crowd and traffic control, and public show.

Cavalry

Cavalry horses are always in the public eye, either marching or on guard. Many are riding horses, but others pull carriages and guns.

Farm

Horses are still widely used on farms—especially in Amish communities—though less now than they used to be. They are used in teams or by themselves, and can work on land that is unsuitable for machinery.

A circus Liberty horse in action.

Horses in Sport

Show jumping

Show jumping is a very popular sport with riders and spectators alike. It can be the local small-fence course where every clear round wins a prize. Or it can be the major international competition where huge cash prizes are won by the best.

The jumping is done in a ring over a series of knock-down fences. The aim is to jump clear. Competitors who knock down fences are given faults (penalties). If more than one rider cleared, there is a jump-off. If this is against the clock, the rider with the fastest round with the least faults wins.

Types of show jumps include uprights, spreads, parallels, and hog's backs. There are many variations.

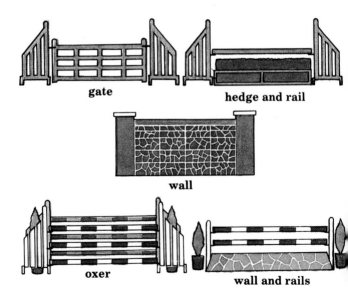

gate

hedge and rail

wall

oxer

wall and rails

Cross-country and eventing

Galloping and jumping cross-country is exciting for horse and rider. Many competitions go all out for it.

Hunter trials are timed events over natural rustic fences. Usually, there are sections for novice and advanced horses, or for riders of different age groups.

The sport of eventing combines a stiff cross-country course with dressage and show jumping. It is the supreme test for endurance, obedience, and jumping abilities of the horse and the skill of the rider. The horse that does well cross-country must also be able to do a calm and accurate dressage test and show-jumping round to win.

Dressage

Great dressage is an art—like ballet on horseback. The French word means "training of a riding horse." The riders guide their horses through a series of paces, using mainly leg and seat signals. The horse should

A show jumper clears a fence in fine style.

59

move smoothly and precisely.

Among the variations to these paces are the extended movements (longer-striding) and collected (shorter-striding). Other movements are rein-back, counter canter, flying change, shoulder-in, *pirouette, piaffé,* and passage.

Driving

There is a worldwide revival in driving. It is no longer simply a way of traveling, but a great equestrian sport. It ranges from small single-pony turnouts to the swift multihorse team, competing internationally in the three-event trials called "combined driving."

Showing

Showing is one way of ensuring that breeds and types of horses and ponies remain as true and as beautiful as they should be.

Competition is fierce in show rings all over the world. Young stock and stallions are shown in-hand (led).

It takes an expert driver (whip) to handle big teams of horses. But single horses or ponies hitched to small vehicles, such as this one, can be driven even by beginners.

A horse being shown in-hand. Everything depends on conformation, fitness, good condition, grooming, and general behavior.

Riding horses and ponies are shown under saddle (ridden). Driving animals are hitched to their vehicles and driven. The show horse should always be a picture of health, spotlessly clean, and well-behaved.

Racing

There are two main types of racing—flat racing and steeplechasing. The Syrians and Arabs held races more than 2,000 years ago.

Flat racing—without fences—began in Britain as early as the tenth century, but didn't become popular until the 1500's. Now it is an established sport, run on about two miles of dirt or turf tracks. Race horses—Thoroughbreds being the best—are worth millions of dollars.

In a steeplechase, the three-mile or longer race includes fences and other obstacles. It is primarily a British sport. Horses are not necessarily as well-bred as those raced on the track. Probably the toughest timber course in the world is the Maryland Cup. It is four miles and over twenty-two fences. Another great race is the Grand National in England.

Polo

Polo is an ancient game played fast and furiously. It looks rather like hockey on horseback.

Teams of players use mallets to try to knock the wooden ball into the goal. The horses' legs are often bandaged. This protects them from swinging mallets.

Hunting

Hunting is popular in the United States, Germany, Ireland, Australia, New Zealand, and France. It is an institution in Britain.

There are various types of hunting: fox, deer, rabbit, and drag (an object pulled over the ground to leave a scented trail). Foxhounds are used for the fox and deer, and beagles and basset hounds hunt the rabbit.

Horses used by hunters must be bold, safe, experienced, and trustworthy so that their riders can concentrate on the task of hunting.

Index